Old RIDDRIE, MILLERSTON and

by
John Hood

Riddrie Knowes is a rocky outcrop of high ground situated to the east of Cumbernauld Road, which must have afforded magnificent views of Glasgow and the surrounding countryside prior to the area's development. Indeed, before 1900 the area was almost completely devoid of houses, the exception being Gartcraig House to the east of the Knowes. In the early 1900s a row of large red sandstone villas was erected on the north side of the drive leading to Gartcraig House, and in this photograph some of these villas (including Larchfield and Knoweside) can be glimpsed through the trees. Until the 1960s, when Glasgow Corporation built further housing on the Knowes, the road to Gartcraig House remained private, hence the 'No Trespassers' signs on the pillars (which have now been demolished). The road in the foreground was formerly known as Cumbernauld Road, but following realignment in the 1920s became Smithycroft Road.

© John Hood 2001
First published in the United Kingdom, 2001,
by Stenlake Publishing, Ochiltree Sawmill, The Lade,
Ochiltree, Ayrshire, KA18 2NX
Telephone / Fax: 01290 423114
www.stenlake.co.uk

ISBN 1 84033 148 8

FURTHER READING

The books listed below were used by the author during his research. With the exception of *Lanarkshire's Mining Legacy*, none of them are available from Stenlake Publishing, and those interested in finding out more are advised to contact their local bookshop or reference library.

Bunyan, Freda and Kidd, Neil (1996), *The Story of Stepps*, Strathkelvin District Libraries & Museums.

Carvel, John L. (1930), *By Glasgow Bus*, Wilson, Guthrie & Co.

Cunnison, J. and Gilfillan, J.B.S. eds (1958), *The Third Statistical Account of Scotland, The City of Glasgow*, Collins.

Eyre-Todd, George (1905), *Official Guide to Glasgow and its Neighbourhood by the Tramway Routes*, Glasgow Corporation Tramways.

Hutton, Guthrie (1993), *Monkland: The Canal That Made Money*, Stenlake Publishing (out of print).

Hutton, Guthrie (1997), *Lanarkshire's Mining Legacy*, Stenlake Publishing.

Kearns, Joe (1992), *Robroyston Hospital 1917–1977*.

Martin, Don (1981), *The Garnkirk & Glasgow Railway*, Strathkelvin District Libraries and Museums.

Peter, Bruce (1996), *100 Years of Glasgow's Amazing Cinemas*, Polygon.

Thomson, George (ed.) (1960), *The Third Statistical Account of Scotland, The County of Lanark*, Collins.

This postcard is captioned 'Blue Bell Dell, Stepps'. Some older residents recall a bluebell dell within the grounds of Garnkirk House (now the clubhouse at Crow Wood Golf Course), but whether this is the one pictured here is not known.

INTRODUCTION

At one time the area covered by this book was entirely comprised of church lands, controlled initially by the Bishop of Glasgow and, later, by the Prebendary, a church official who ranked second only to the Bishop himself. His full title was the Prebendary Canon of Barlanark and probably the most famous of these prebendaries was King James IV. The principal residence of the Prebendary Canons of Barlanark was Provan Hall, which lies to the east of Hogganfield. In addition they maintained a town house, Provand's Lordship, built in 1471 by Bishop Andrew Muirhead and now the oldest house in Glasgow. After the Reformation the church lands were broken up and split into estates. From the 1890s onwards, these were (with the exception of Stepps) disjoined from Cadder Parish and brought within the City of Glasgow's boundaries. Blackhill, for example, was annexed by the Corporation in 1899, to be followed by Robroyston and Millerston in 1926, Hogganfield in 1931, and Cardowan in 1938.

Until the 1800s, farming was the predominant activity in the area, and what little industry there was comprised mostly quarrying, bleaching, and fireclay and ice manufacturing. The first signs of more major industrialisation came with the opening in 1770 of the Monkland Canal and, a decade later, the construction of a major turnpike road connecting Glasgow with Edinburgh and Stirling. The former was built to transport coal from the Monkland collieries and foreshadowed the opening in 1831 of the Garnkirk & Glasgow Railway, which was also primarily constructed for this purpose. Both the canal and railway were supported by local landowners but initially neither development had much effect on the district's population. When a passenger train station was opened in Stepps, for instance, wealthy Glasgow merchants were initially reluctant to settle in the area, despite the advantages of country living with easy access to the city.

By the beginning of the twentieth century, therefore, much of the area still comprised open fields and farmland and was largely the haunt of the rambler! Robroyston – with its historical connection with Sir William Wallace – was a popular destination, but the numerous guidebooks issued at that time also proclaimed the beauty of Provanmill and Millerston. The impetus for development eventually came from Glasgow with the opening in 1882 of Barlinnie Prison in what later became Riddrie, and the establishment of Robroyston Hospital in 1917. These developments, coupled shortly afterwards with substantial housebuilding programmes at Riddrie and Blackhill, when Glasgow's post-war slum clearance programme commenced, made significant inroads into the green belt. Other major developments included the opening in the 1920s of Hogganfield Park and Cardowan Colliery, the former coinciding with the extension of the Glasgow Corporation tramway system to Millerston. Further change ensued and by the 1930s the Monkland Canal had become disused (it was latterly filled in to provide the foundation for the new M8 motorway), trams ceased running in 1962, and a new Stepps bypass (the M80) was constructed on the fields of Robroyston. Other changes include the closure of Robroyston Hospital and Cardowan Colliery, and, last but not least, the magnificent tearoom at Hogganfield, where uniformed waitresses once sedately served teas!

Although Garfield House, built in the late 1800s, has been greatly extended over the years, the original structure is still recognisable. Prior to the 1960s when it became Garfield House Hotel, it had had several well-known owners. One such was William B. Ross, convenor of the building committee for Stepps Parish Church, and a motivating force behind the establishment of the church. A member of Stepps and Chryston Golf Club, he formally opened the club in November 1900. Other owners included J. Raeside Auld, a Lanark County Councillor, who commissioned a major refurbishment of the house in 1902, and David Pollock Smith, Councillor and Deputy Lord Lieutenant of Lanarkshire from 1935 to 1961. Visitors to the house during Pollock Smith's ownership included a Glasgow businessman, William Watt, who was accused by Peter Manuel of the murder of Mr Watt's wife, sister-in-law and daughter. Manuel was himself ultimately convicted of these murders.

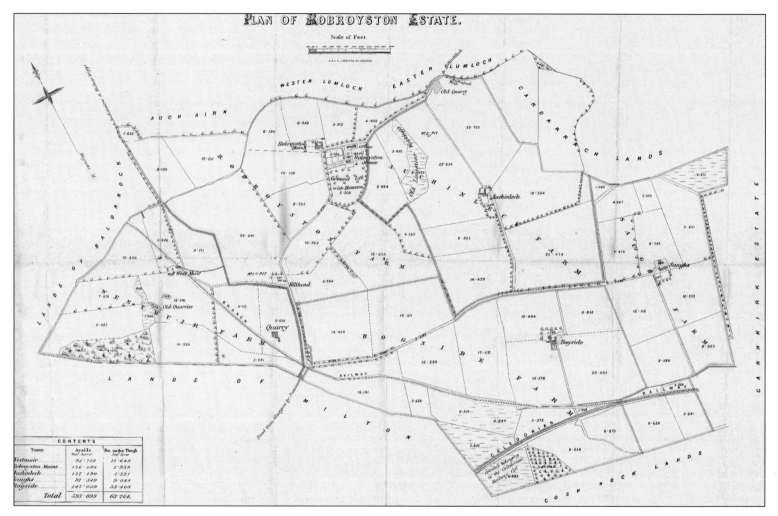

PLAN OF ROBROYSTON ESTATE.

Robroyston was once a small estate within the Parish of Cadder. In the 1600s it was owned by the Hamilton family, but from the 1890s onwards the Corporation of Glasgow began to acquire parts of the estate, which at that time comprised Robroyston House, five farms, a brickworks, an ironstone pit and a quarry. In 1908, 153 acres of the estate were sold by the Corporation's Cleansing Department to Glasgow's Health Board for the site of an infectious diseases hospital. By then referred to as the 'City of Glasgow's estate', Robroyston was formally brought within the city boundaries in 1926.

In the late 1880s the Glasgow District Board of Lunacy advertised for a site for their new lunatic asylum, specifying that the ideal site should be no more than 12 miles outside Glasgow city boundary and should comprise 350 acres of land and a farm. Robroyston was one of four sites considered, the others being Auchinloch, Crookston and Gartloch. In the event the Gartloch site was chosen and the asylum was opened there on 3 June 1897.

SCHEDULE of INFORMATION wished by the SUB-COMMITTEE ON LAND of the GLASGOW DISTRICT BOARD OF LUNACY, in reference to the Estate of *Robroyston*

1. Name and general Description of Property and Situation?	Robroyston situated about three miles North east from Glasgow Exchange. The ground undulating & commands fine views of the surrounding country. The soil produces good crops. The estate is divided into five farms. The gradients are easy.
2. Extent of Ground?	about 680 acres
3. Extents of Arable Land, Wooded Land, Moorland, and other Ground making up the Total?	all arable except about 20 to 25 acres Moss land which can be Reclaimed
4. Description of Buildings at present on Ground?	A Mansion House & offices & five farm steadings. The Mansion House old, the steadings in good repair.
5. Lowest Price?	A tentative offer of £85,000 Stg made to the Board
6. Rate per Acre?	£125 Stg per acre including minerals.
7. Amount of Feu-duty?	Nil. Some small feu duties are received.
8. Amount of other Burdens?	See particulars in offer made by Davidson & Syme W.S on 29th Novr 1881
9. Are Minerals reserved or included?	Included
10. Duration of existing Leases (if any)?	Particulars in letter of Davidson & Syme W.S referred to above.
11. Water Supply? (Particulars as to nature, extent, and means of Supply).	Loch Katrine Water supplies the villages of Millerston Provan Mill & Auchenairn on the borders of the estate. Good springs are abundant on the estate
12. Gas Supply?	Nil
13. Sewage?	Nil. There are two burns flowing through the estate
14. Nearest Stone Quarry?	On the lands. There are also old limestone workings on the estate
15. Name of nearest Railway Station, and distance therefrom?	Steppes about 1/4 of a mile
16. Does Railway pass through Land, or could Siding on Property be arranged for?	Main line of Caledonian intersects the estate. There is also a Branch line in connection with iron stone pit & quarry.
17. Distance by Rail from Glasgow?	3½ Miles
18. Number of Trains per day?	20 trains going & returning.
19. Average time taken by Trains from Glasgow to nearest Station?	10 minutes to Steppes. Caledonian Railway have taken off ground for a station which it is believed they are willing to erect as soon as a public work or institution is erected. This would bring the estate within 6 or 7 minutes of Buchanan St Station.
20. Any other Particulars which it occurs to the Proprietors to communicate?	If only 3 or 400 acres are wanted by the Board the proprietors are willing to treat for this quantity.
21. Name and Address of Agents or Proprietors to whom Communications to be addressed?	Davidson & Syme W.S. 22 Castle St Edinburgh. Donald McCorquodale 16 Hope St Glasgow acts as factor & will hold himself in readiness to point out the Boundaries of the estate any time the Board of Lunacy may appoint.

5

This North-Eastern Automobile Co. Ltd. garage occupied a very prominent corner site at the junction of Cumbernauld Road and Edinburgh Road. Trading from the late 1920s until the mid-1950s, the garage was also used as an ambulance depot during the Second World War. Today the petrol pumps in the foreground have gone, but the garage (albeit slightly altered in appearance) remains and is now used as a tyre and exhaust centre.

From the 1930s, Riddrie cinema-goers were well-served by two superb 'state of the art' cinemas: the Rex and the Riddrie Picture House, opened in 1931 and 1938 respectively. In this late 1950's view of Cumbernauld Road, the latter can be seen on the right, behind the city-bound Coronation tram. The area's other cinema, the Rex, was particularly striking in its design and was later used as a model for other British suburban cinemas. Gradually, however, as with cinemas throughout the country, the Rex lost some of its appeal, and despite refurbishment and a change of name to the ABC in 1961, the decline in patron numbers ultimately resulted in its closure in September 1973. Later the Rex was pulled down and the site redeveloped. A car showroom now stands in its place. Also visible in the photograph are the single-storey Quick Cup transport café (to the near left) and, in the distance, the red sandstone tenements at Dee Street.

Part of the frontage of the stunning Riddrie Picture House can be seen in this 1958 view of Cumbernauld Road at its junction with Dee Street and Warriston Street. This cinema (along with the nearby Parade Cinema in Alexandra Parade) was owned by two Glasgow Councillors, George Smith and James Welsh. The Riddrie Picture House was formally opened on 7 February 1938 by Sir John Stewart, Lord Provost of Glasgow. With the balcony seats reserved for invited guests, the proprietors were free to charge admission to the stalls for those citizens who wished to get a glimpse of their Lord Provost! Like the nearby Rex, the Riddrie Picture House was initially well-patronised. However, despite a change of ownership and name (it became the Vogue in 1950), a decline in audience numbers ultimately led to its closure as a cinema. Unlike the Rex, however, the then owner, George Singleton, converted the Picture House into a bingo hall in 1968, thereby avoiding the loss of this magnificent art deco structure, the exterior of which remains little changed today.

In 1914 three blocks of red sandstone tenements were erected on the west side of Cumbernauld Road: this photograph shows the block that stands between Gough Street and Gadie Street. To the rear of the tenements was an open area known as the 'back field', where generations of Riddrie youngsters congregated to play games such as kick-the-can and football. The single-storey property beyond the tenement is the lodge of Blackhill House. From there an avenue led directly north to the house, a rather plain-looking two-storey property once owned by a Mr Martin (a Glasgow pins and needles manufacturer). Alongside the house were some low whitewashed farm buildings. The lands on which the house stood were within the Barony of Provan, once owned by Sir Robert Hamilton of Silverhill. In 1875 they were purchased by the Corporation of Glasgow from the then owner, Robert Walker of Lethamhill. When the new Kennyhill and Riddrie housing estate was built, Blackhill House was demolished.

A 1950's view of Cumbernauld Road with Riddrie St Thomas' Church in the foreground. Built in 1957, it is, with the exception of the steeple (which burnt down in the 1970s), largely unchanged today. The church lies within the parish of St Thomas', which was established in the 1920s to serve the new Kennyhill and Riddrie housing estate. Until a church was built in 1924, a private house (Rosemount) was used by the congregation for worship. The 1924 church is now used as the church hall and its entrance can be seen to the right, just north of Longford Street. A prominent feature of the present-day church is the large mural of the Apostle Thomas which adorns the south-west wall. Beyond St Thomas', on the other side of Smithycroft Road, lies St Enoch's Hogganfield Church of Scotland. The parish of St Enoch was one of the five original Glasgow parishes and was centred around St Enoch Square – Enoch being a corruption of Thenew, the mother of Glasgow's patron saint, St Mungo. When the original St Enoch's Church in Glasgow city centre was demolished the parish was transferred to Riddrie.

In this late 1950's view the first of the two Standard trams is passing Lethamhill Road en route to the centre of Glasgow. In the main, the properties to left of the picture have survived, but most of those opposite, including the whitewashed Maxwellton Cottage, have been replaced by newer housing. Milk was once sold from this cottage, and the area behind it (known locally as The Orchard) was used by the Cadona family to park their fairground caravans. The tenement partially obscured by the near tram lay derelict for many years and became a popular haunt for local children. In the far distance a Coronation tram is standing at Riddrie terminus, with the Lethamhill Terrace tenements on Gartloch Road visible beyond it.

This view of Smithycroft Road shows the Riddrie tram terminus, which was situated at Naver Street and included a cross-over facility, thus enabling trams to change tracks to make the return journey to the city centre. On 1 November 1959 the No. 6 Riddrie–Scotstoun tram service ceased and trolley buses were introduced. To the left of the Coronation tram can be seen a small, square, brick-built communal air raid shelter. This was provided during the Second World War for residents who didn't have an Anderson shelter in their garden. Although the shelter was retained after the war, it was eventually demolished. A modern church of the Congregation of Riddrie Jehovah's Witnesses now stands at the corner of Teith Street. The shops, Masonic Lodge and bungalow on the right of picture have all survived, although the two-storey building beyond, which once housed prison officers, has been replaced by new housing. The open fields to the south of Lethamhill Terrace are now occupied by Smithycroft Secondary School, which opened on 23 February 1968. Today Smithycroft Road is closed off at this point.

In this late 1950's view the Coronation tram is city-bound, having just changed lines at the terminus cross-over at Naver Street. The shops to the left of the picture once included a branch of the Shettleston Co-operative Society (later Cochrane, the grocers) and Walter Hubbard's bakery. The Riddrievale Street tenement beyond the shops was demolished in the 1970s and replaced with new housing. Houses now stand on the vacant ground at the corner of Teith Street. The roof of Young Brothers' haulage yard can be glimpsed towards the foot of Smithycroft Road.

Barlinnie Prison, which was opened in 1882, was built on a greenfield site to the north-east of Glasgow in what is now Riddrie. Prior to its opening male prisoners were held at Duke Street Prison, which then became a women's prison. Up until 1928 all executions were carried out at Duke Street, but thereafter they took place within Barlinnie. Undoubtedly the most notorious prisoner to be hanged in the modern era was Peter Manuel, who was convicted of the murder of seven people, and in 1958 was one of the last people to be hanged in Scotland. In front of the prison is the Monkland Canal, once the busiest canal in Scotland. It was constructed principally to transport coal to Glasgow from collieries in the Monklands area. Work on the canal began in 1770 under the direction of James Watt, but progress was slow and by 1773, when Watt left the project, the canal had only reached a temporary terminus near Barlinnie Prison. In 1789, with a change of ownership and an injection of fresh capital, the canal was extended to Townhead in Glasgow. By the late 1800s, however, much of the area's coal was being transported by rail so that by 1930 the canal had become largely disused. It was finally abandoned in the 1950s and was filled in a decade later.

From 1789 until 1794 there was effectively a 'gap' in the Monkland Canal at Blackhill: one part of it finished on a hill 96 feet above another stretch at the foot of the hill. This meant that barges had to be unloaded at the top of the hill and the coal put into wagons, before being reloaded onto barges at the foot of the hill. As traffic on the canal increased this operation became less viable, so in 1794 a series of four double locks was constructed. These were rebuilt in 1841 to cope with a further increase in use. However, within a decade the locks had become a bottleneck again, due to the ever-increasing traffic. The solution was provided by a Glasgow engineer, James Leslie, and in 1850 Scotland's only 'inclined plane' (seen here to the right of the whitewashed Blackhill Cottage) was brought into operation. This allowed the empty barges to be hauled up the hill on iron caissons. However, by 1887 the amount of traffic on the canal had decreased and the inclined plane was abandoned.

Prior to 1869, Glasgow citizens received their gas supply from either the Glasgow Gas Light Company, or the City and Suburban Gas Company of Glasgow. In that year, however, Glasgow Corporation sought parliamentary powers to take over the two private gas companies, and erect a municipal gas works. Although the former was accepted, the latter was refused, and the Corporation were therefore obliged to utilise existing private gasworks at Townhead, Partick, Dalmarnock and Tradeston. However, these soon proved inadequate to meet demand, and new gasworks were eventually built at Dawsholm and Provan. The Provan gasworks were initially proposed in 1898, when a 123 acre site was purchased. This lay partly on Easter Blochairn, and the Blackhill and Germiston estates. The new works were officially opened on 14 September 1904. When the gas industry was nationalised, Provan gasworks were transferred to the Scottish Gas Board. On 11 August 1958, Glasgow's Lord Provost, Sir Myer Galpern, inaugurated a £2 million modernisation of the works, making them then the largest producer and distributor of gas in Scotland, capable of delivering 40 million cubic feet of gas daily.

Today the most prominent feature of the now defunct Provan gasworks is the two 280-foot diameter, three-lift gasometers. Each capable of holding over eight million cubic feet of gas, when built they were the largest of their kind in Scotland. However, many of the gasworks buildings have now been demolished, including the 400-foot long coal store and the retort houses. The former could hold 50,000 tons of coal and was situated on higher ground to the rear of the works. This elevation enabled coal wagons to be brought into the coal store on a platform 17 feet above floor level. From there, the coal was tipped into a service hopper, where it was broken up. The coal was then taken by an 800-foot long conveyor to higher level storage hoppers, before being fed into the retort, where it was burnt. The resultant gas was then piped to the gasometer for storage, while the left over coke fell through openings in the floor of the retort house onto tipping wagons below, and was then taken to the nearby coke stackyards.

When Barlinnie Prison was first built there was an immediate need for staff housing, and blocks of sandstone tenements were built on Lethamhill Road, just outside the south walls of the prison. There were vegetable plots in front of these buildings, and older Riddrie residents still remember prisoners being allowed 'out' to tend the plots. In the 1970s the tenements were replaced with modern Corporation maisonettes. The prison governor was provided with a separate house, which was shown on local maps as 'Governor's House'. This was situated to the east of the prison, in what is now Lethamhill Crescent. In later years some of the prison officers were housed in Smithycroft Road.

Although the old Cumbernauld Road had been realigned, the new section from St Thomas' Church to Smithycroft Bridge was too steep for tramway operations, therefore trams such as this Standard No. 12 on route 7 continued to use Smithycroft Road. The roofs of houses in Gala Street can be seen to the extreme left of the tram, along with Mackay's tearoom. This single-storey building had space inside for little more than two small tables, but was always well patronised – the customers being attracted by the tearoom's hot peas and vinegar or sweets and ice cream. Smithycroft Bridge, named after Smithy Croft Cottage, (which is out of shot on the opposite bank of the canal), can just be seen to the rear of the tram. When first constructed the bridge would have been built to the canal company's specifications, with stone abutments and timber decking. However, the original bridge was replaced in 1923 with a much sturdier structure and the tramway line was extended to Millerston the following year.

Gala Street, Riddrie. No. 3.

The Kennyhill and Riddrie housing estate, which includes Gala Street, was the first scheme undertaken by Glasgow Corporation following the passing of the 1919 Addison Act, which enabled local authorities to provide better accommodation for working class tenants. Not surprisingly, there was a huge waiting list of prospective tenants. In total 1,000 houses were built between 1920 and 1927 on open fields to the west of Cumbernauld Road. By all accounts the scheme was filled with 'a better class of tenant', and indeed a contemporary letter in a local newspaper humorously referred to Riddrie as the 'intellectual suburb' on account of the presence of several community and church groups. The scheme consisted of 50% semi-detached properties and 50% tenements; the latter (albeit with cheaper rents) lacking such things as front gates and back gardens. A serious concern at the time was that the houses had been built on high ground and therefore were badly affected by inclement weather. In the 1980s the houses on the north side of Gala Street, from No. 47 onwards, were demolished to allow construction of the M8 motorway.

Lethamhill Terrace (known locally as Foote's Building) occupied a prominent position at the corner of Cumbernauld Road and Gartloch Road. Built by Mr Foote, a businessman who lived in nearby Laura Cottage, Lethamhill Terrace was a red sandstone building comprising nineteen flats with two ground floor shops. One of these was a cobblers and the other was the well-known Golfers Rest Café (also known as Paddy's). Until 1929 the café was owned by the Italian Paddy Di'Mascio, but when he opened another café near the Millerston tram terminus it was acquired by a Mr Bremner. On Mr Bremner's retirement in 1944, the business was taken over for a few years by Mr Foote's son, who then sold it to Antonio Capaldi. By all accounts the café sold the most delicious ice cream and was much frequented by local children, and golfers playing on the nearby golf course. Lethamhill Terrace and the surrounding buildings were demolished to make way for the M8 motorway.

In the late nineteenth century Glasgow's ice industry was centred around Hogganfield Loch, with several ice houses clustered around it supplying ice to the city's shops. The loch, which is the source of the Molendinar Burn, was also popular with skaters and curlers in winter. It was therefore perhaps not surprising that Glasgow Corporation began to acquire the land around the loch with the intention of constructing a public park. From 1912 onwards the Corporation bought ground for this purpose, although some local landowners were reluctant to sell and it was not until July 1924 that the park was officially opened. To coincide with this event the Corporation tramway network was extended to Millerston, allowing trams to proceed beyond the original terminus on Naver Street, Riddrie, over the new Smithycroft Bridge and past Hogganfield Loch to the terminus in Station Road, Millerston.

When Hogganfield Park was first laid out around Hogganfield Loch in 1924, special provision was made for boaters. The loch itself extends to 50 acres and easily accommodated the two motor launches and 100 rowing boats then provided by Glasgow Corporation for recreational use. The park was once crowded at weekends with families spending time rowing on the loch, and was also popular with courting couples, who earned Hogganfield Loch the name the 'winching loch'! The tearoom, which was opened at the same time as the park, initially proved very popular, but was latterly mainly used by golfers on the adjacent Lethamhill golf course who would breakfast there before teeing off. Eventually it was closed and, although several entrepreneurs attempted to revive it, they were unsuccessful. There are no longer any boats on Hogganfield Loch, although since 1968 the park has operated as a local nature reserve, and is currently home to 127 different species of waterfowl.

With the exception of Millerston United Free Church (seen here on the north side of Cumbernauld Road), all the other buildings in this photograph have been demolished. The church (which dates from 1856) is largely unchanged today and still contains a small upper balcony which was built to accommodate boys from the nearby Mossbank Industrial School. Access to the balcony was (and still is) by a set of stairs located immediately inside the front entrance, thus ensuring complete segregation of the boys from the rest of the congregation. To the west of the church the old Garngad Road (now Royston Road) led to the district known as Garngad (modern-day Royston). Until the 1970s the open fields to the left of Garngad Road were used by the Pinkerton family to grow vast quantities of rhubarb. These rhubarb fields were an irresistible magnet for generations of Garngad youngsters, who would go there by what became known as the 'Rhubarb Fields Road', to pick stalks of rhubarb to dip into bags of sugar, which they brought with them from home. Private housing now stands on the site of the rhubarb fields.

Mossbank School, Millerston.

Mossbank Industrial School was situated to the north of Cumbernauld Road, halfway between Millerston United Free Church and Robroyston station. The school was opened in 1869 by the Glasgow Juvenile Delinquency Board and was for boys only. The initial intakes were apparently completely lacking in discipline and were described in a local newspaper as 'wild colts'. The length of time that pupils spent at the school varied, but their stay was used to reform their characters. Later, with the establishment of the Glasgow School Board, it was said that new pupils were slightly more disciplined. Nonetheless, one visitor to the school reported that the boys were more inclined to leave the buildings by climbing down the rone pipes than by the doors! In addition to instilling discipline in them, the school encouraged the youngsters to better their education, so much so that by the beginning of the nineteenth century all of the then 28 pupils were attending technical college.

Although Glasgow's boundaries were not extended to include Robroyston until 1926, the Corporation had already acquired some land there by the late 1800s. Therefore, when proposals to build an infectious diseases hospital were first put forward in 1890, Robroyston was seen as suitable for the purpose. It was not the first choice: in the early stages of the proposal a site was identified alongside Barlinnie Prison, but this was shelved because of local objections. The new hospital finally opened in 1917, but was immediately commandeered by the government as a military hospital. In 1919 Robroyston Hospital was returned to the local health board and, although initially serving as an infectious diseases hospital, it eventually dealt with maternity, geriatric, orthopaedic and paediatric cases. On 5 January 1976 the Greater Glasgow Health Board announced the intended closure of the hospital, citing a falling population and the need for major remedial building work as the main factors in their decision. The hospital closed in 1977 and today some 600 private houses stand on its site.

When Robroyston Hospital was built it was encircled by a belt of trees, presumably in an effort to camouflage and shelter it. Erected on a greenfield site and surrounded on all sides by open fields, access for staff and visitors was always difficult. In order to alleviate the problem for the former, a large nurses' home was built at the western edge of the complex, facing directly onto Robroyston Road. Visitors had to use either the bus or tram, and in 1950 Glasgow Corporation agreed to provide a bus shelter, since as many as twelve buses could be parked at the nearby terminus at any given time. The journey by tram involved walking from Millerston terminus across the fields to the hospital, either by way of Station Road and Bogside Road, or by using a right of way which ran past Mossbank Industrial School. Some patients also had quite a journey to Robroyston Hospital, for whilst it was in use as a military hospital wounded soldiers were brought to Robroyston station by train and then transferred to the hospital by ambulance.

Wallace's Well, Robroyston, near Lenzie

Wallace's Well and nearby monument were frequently mentioned in publications listing pleasant walks and rambles in the vicinity of Glasgow. They also appeared in guidebooks issued by Glasgow Corporation to encourage people to use their tramway system for leisure pursuits. In these booklets, readers were urged to take the No. 8 tram to Millerston and walk across the fields past Bogside and Auchinleck Farms to see the well and monument. Clearly, many did so! However, there were some who disputed the historical association of the well, and one old local map refers to it simply as Auchinleck Well. A historian writing in 1907 also noted that the respected author and historian, Hugh MacDonald, made no mention of the well in his *Rambles Round Glasgow*, published in 1854 to encourage people to visit places of historical interest. Notwithstanding this, there is no doubt that a visit to the well was a popular outing. In addition, local children playing in the nearby woods used it to quench their thirst.

Wallace's Well, where local tradition says William Wallace came to drink, lies to the east of the Wallace Monument. In the last hundred years not only has its position changed (apparently it was moved by the owners of Auchinleck Farm from the left side of the nearby burn to its present position on the right side), but its appearance has been considerably altered. An early line drawing by the historian and writer T. C. F. Brotchie, in his *Some Sylvan Scenes Round Glasgow*, depicts the well as a small pool with a barred brick structure behind it, an image that is in complete contrast to the above photograph. Today the well has been further altered and a new pink granite lintel added bearing the legend 'Wallace's Well'.

Historians have speculated that the name Robroyston derives from 'Ralph Raa's toun', Ralph Raa being the Ralph de Haliburton who was recruited by Sir John Menteith to help capture Sir William Wallace. According to Blind Harry's *Life of Wallace* (published in 1450), Wallace was captured in 1305 by Menteith while sheltering with a servant in a house in 'Rabreaeston' (Robroyston). This monument, a granite Celtic cross, was erected in 1900 on or near the spot where the house stood until its demolition c.1826. It is said that a Kirkintilloch customs official and antiquarian, on hearing of the impending demolition, rescued some of the oak rafters. He had these fashioned into an armchair, which he presented to the novelist Sir Walter Scott. In 1986, under Glasgow's 'Adopt a Monument' scheme, the category 'B' listed cross was adopted by the Clan Wallace Society in America, who donated £1,700 for its restoration and for landscaping works.

Until 1926, when Glasgow's boundaries were extended to include it, the village of Millerston had been within the Barony Parish of Lanarkshire. The original village was initially located further west alongside the quite separate Hogganfield village, but by the 1950s (when this photograph was taken) Millerston had developed further east along Cumbernauld Road, at its junction with Station Road and Avenue End Road. Apart from the removal of the tramway lines and overhead cables little has changed, and today all the properties seen to the left of the picture still stand, although McKenzie's grocers (with the awning) is now Alex McKay's public house, The Real McKay. Since 1954, the space at the corner of Avenue End Road (formerly the site of Paddy Di'Mascio's café) has been occupied by the New Inn public house.

Robroyston station was one of several intermediate stations on the former Garnkirk & Glasgow Railway line which, like the Monkland Canal, was laid primarily to carry coal from the Monklands collieries to Glasgow. Laying the stretch of line at Robroyston posed particular problems for the contractors, since it crossed Robroyston Moss, and to support the track red pine planks had to be laid on top of Scotch pine sleepers. Although primarily a freight line, it also provided a rudimentary passenger service for the nearby community of Millerston, although as Robroyston station was some distance away commuters had quite a walk to reach it. In July 1844 the Garnkirk & Glasgow Railway Co. was absorbed into the Glasgow, Garnkirk & Coatbridge Railway Co., which in turn was eventually taken over by the Caledonian Railway Co. Ultimately the line became part of the British Rail network and Robroyston station was closed to passengers on 11 June 1956. Today all that remains is a metal latticed footbridge.

Around 1910 the property known as Mossvale, which was located to the west of Station Road, Millerston, comprised some farm buildings and a rather grand-looking Scots baronial tower house. By the 1930s, however, the farm buildings had been demolished and the property left standing was simply called The Tower. This was in fact a nineteenth century reconstruction of a typical seventeenth century tower house. Although now a category 'B' listed building, it lay derelict for many years and until recently was situated in a scrap merchant's yard. When the business was sold, the land was acquired by a major housebuilder, who is currently restoring The Tower and building flats on the site of the old farm buildings. Also visible in this photograph, in the distance, beyond Station Road, is Coshneuk Farm. Although the farm buildings are still standing, they are now used by the local authority as a works depot.

Station Road, Millerston

Station Road, Millerston, was formed following the opening of the Garnkirk & Glasgow Railway to provide access to Robroyston station from Cumbernauld Road. Other than the farm-steading at Mossvale, there was originally no housing on Station Road – the houses which now stand on the north side of Station Road (including Craigbarnet Crescent) weren't built until the 1920s, and even then didn't run the full length of the road. In recent years substantial building has taken place behind Station Road.

When the Corporation tramway system was extended to Millerston in 1924 a new terminus, complete with turning facility, was established on Station Road. In this late 1950's view a city-bound Coronation tram is turning right into Cumbernauld Road. Following it is an older Standard tram. The journey from Millerston to the city took approximately half an hour. At its peak, Glasgow's tramway system was second in size only to the London County Council system, and until 1954 trams were even colour-coded by route for the convenience of users. In 1957, however, a decision was taken to gradually phase out the trams in favour of trolley buses. Accordingly, on 14 March 1959, shortly after this photograph was taken, the No. 8 Millerston–Rouken Glen–Giffnock Road service was withdrawn. Trams, or 'shugglies' as they were affectionately known, hold a special place in the memory of many, and when tramway services in Glasgow finally ceased on 4 September 1962, some 250,000 spectators packed into Glasgow's Argyle Street to see the last shugglie pass by.

Stepps Farm (later known as Steppshill Farm) was one of five farms on the former Garnkirk Estate, the others being Whitehill, Auchengree, Gateside and Hornshill. Stepps Farm was located on Cumbernauld Road, to the west of Laundry Lane. It is shown on maps dated 1914 as Steepshill Farm, but by the 1930s the farmlands appear to have gone, leaving a property known as Steppshill Farm House surrounded on three sides by housing. The last owner of the house (Mrs Zacarrini) sold it in 1959, after which it was demolished and a supermarket built on the site and that of an adjacent garage. Almost directly opposite Steppshill Farm House was Steppshill Terrace, behind which was a pony trotting track. This track (known locally as Marshall Park) was laid out in the 1940s on ground that once formed part of Frankfield Loch. Owned by Ralph Marshall, the track was later sold to a Carluke car dealer, Allan Gray, who renamed it Stepps Stadium. The track grandstand was built using surplus war materials and the track was strengthened during construction with ashes from the now defunct Provan gasworks. When pony trotting ceased, stock car racing was introduced, but the stadium was ultimately closed and the site cleared.

Whitehill Avenue boasts the oldest house in Stepps – Mark Brae – which was built in 1855 and is situated at what is now the junction of Cumbernauld Road and Whitehill Avenue. In 1897 a further three houses were built on the avenue, but even so, when the Stepps Established Church (seen here on the left) was opened on 27 May 1900, it stood on a greenfield site. This had been feued by Col. Alexander Sprot of Garnkirk, with only nominal feu-duty charged. Prior to the opening of the church worshippers had to attend Hogganfield Parish Church. Later, 'kitchen meetings' were held in a house in Steppshill, and from 1885 until their new church was opened, in the Union Hall, Cardowan Drive. The church was built of red Ballochmyle sandstone and, since it was to be lit by acetylene gas, provision was made for a gas house to be built at the rear. A hall was added on 12 October 1912 and electricity was introduced into the church and hall in 1928. When the Established and United Free Churches in Scotland reunited in 1929, Stepps Established Church was renamed Whitehill Parish Church.

Whitehill Farm Road stands on the line of an old road that predates the 1780's turnpike road (now Cumbernauld Road). It can be traced from present-day Edward Place, where it turns sharply north along Laundry Lane before heading east past Whitehill Farm and onto Mount Harriet Drive. A stone pillar (complete with metal plaque) on Mount Harriet Drive commemorates the building of the old road, as well as marking the location of a toll gate. The houses in this view have all survived largely unchanged.

The most prominent building at the Cross is the red sandstone structure known locally as Wright's Building. This was erected in 1910 as a family residence by local builder, Harry Wright. The ground floor shop was later run by Miss E. Caldwell and today this is The Moss Newsagent. John Mackenzie's shop (previously William Stein, the grocer) stood opposite in Craigielea Terrace. Ivybank Cottage, beyond Miss Caldwell's shop on Cardowan Drive, was once Glass's newsagent and tobacconist. The present occupant (and, incidentally, the last owner of the shop) has used the cottage as a private residence since 1994.

When the Garnkirk & Glasgow Railway was opened in 1831, a station known as Cumbernauld Road was opened. This was the first intermediate station on the line from Glasgow and remained so until the opening of Robroyston station. The station later became known as Steps Road, and on 1 September 1924, while under the ownership of the London Midland & Scottish Company, the name was changed once more, this time simply to Stepps. On 5 November 1962 the station was closed, but the short stretch of Station Road that leads off Cardowan Drive still remains. The station buildings and platforms have gone, and all that remains is a metal gate and some steps on Cumbernauld Road marking one of the two former access points. Today there is a new passenger station which was opened slightly further along the line on 16 May 1989 and is operated by Strathclyde Passenger Transport Executive.

Cardowan Drive, Stepps.

In 1906, when this photograph was taken, Cardowan Drive was still relatively undeveloped and contained only a few houses built in the 1870s and 1890s. Gas, supplied by Glasgow Corporation, had only just replaced the old paraffin lamps and it would be a few more years before the next spate of house-building would begin in the Drive. A more pressing need for Stepps at this time was a community hall, a requirement that was met in September 1885 when the Union Hall was opened. This building (now Stepps Community Hall) is to the left of the picture, almost at Stepps Cross. Originally used by all the local church groups for Sunday school and temperance meetings etc., it also served temporarily at one time as a school, known as 'the wee school'. Between 1900 and 1906 two churches were built in Stepps and, having become surplus to requirements, the hall was handed over to the Parish Council for secular use.

Many of the houses in Cardowan Drive (seen here looking east towards Cardowan Colliery) have survived largely unchanged. As elsewhere in Stepps, the earliest houses in the street were built for wealthy Glasgow businessmen who chose to work in the city but live in the country. Later, some of the houses were occupied by colliery officials. The old gas lamp on the left-hand side of the street marks the approximate entrance to School Road, where a school was opened on 19 August 1902, replacing the temporary school held in the Union Hall. Prior to this Stepps children (depending on where they lived) attended either Millerston, Auchinloch or Chryston Schools. The new school, Stepps Primary, was extended in January 1911 with the addition of five new classrooms and a schoolmaster's house. It was extensively modernised between 1957 and 1960.

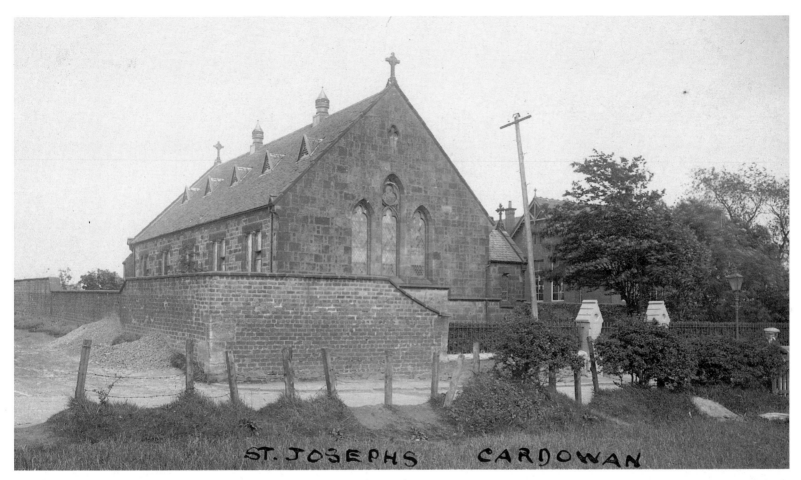

St. Josephs Cardowan

The Church of St Joseph's, Cardowan, was opened on 14 November 1875 by Archbishop Eyre of Glasgow to meet the needs of some 1,000 parishioners from the surrounding villages. The preferred site for the church had been on Cumbernauld Road, but in the event a site on Cardowan Road was chosen. Initially the church was also used as a school (during which time a curtain would be drawn across the sanctuary), with the first classes commencing on 2 August 1880. In 1901 a new purpose-built school was opened alongside the church, but in 1933 this was closed and its pupils transferred to a new St Joseph's School in nearby Muirhead. However, on 9 January 1950 the old school in Cardowan was reopened until a new school was built on playing fields lying opposite. This new school, St Joseph's Primary, was opened on 21 May 1985, after which the old school was taken over by the Diocese of Motherwell for use as a parish centre.

Although coal has been extracted in the Cardowan area since the 1800s, it was not until the early 1920s that the coal reserves were mined extensively. Cardowan Colliery was begun by James Dunlop & Co., who sunk two pits between 1924 and 1928. A decade later, with hundreds of miners being bussed into the area daily, a greenfield site at nearby Craigendmuir was released to build workers' housing. After nationalisation of the coal industry in 1947, a third pit was sunk to tap into the coal reserves to the south of Cardowan. By the 1960s Cardowan was the only working Lanarkshire pit, and narrowly avoided closure (and the loss of 1,400 jobs) in December 1969. Following further reductions in the coal industry, Cardowan Colliery finally closed on 26 August 1983. Shortly afterwards the site was cleared, and a major housing development is currently being built on it.

In this view of Cumbernauld Road looking west, the houses of Dean Terrace and Dundonald Terrace are to the left, with a group of houses and shops between Blenheim Avenue and Lenzie Road standing opposite. Among the latter were the Stepps branch of Gillies the Baker, then Adam McNish (grocers), Sloan (also a grocers, but later Mrs Prentice's sweet shop), and Jean MacKenzie's fruit and vegetable shop. In the next block there was Dr Maguire's surgery, Miss Bannerman's drapery shop, Leiper's fishmonger and, finally, Brown's the butchers. The little cottage with the twin dormers is Groningen, now a private residence but once Hielke Swart's post office. Although the shops have now changed hands the properties themselves remain largely unchanged today.

Main Road, Stepps.

In this 1926 view of Main Road (Cumbernauld Road) looking east, the entire length of Dean Terrace is prominent. The sign at the lane on the right is for Bob Watson's joinery and undertakers' premises which were situated here. The building with the ornamental wrought ironwork (which it still retains), was one of a suite of shops run by Shettleston Co-operative Society. The local telephone exchange was also in Dean Terrace at one time. One of its first transmissions – received in May 1900 – reputedly told of the Relief of Mafeking. On the opposite side of the road Gillies the Bakers can be glimpsed, and beyond it the distinctive turreted building now occupied by the Royal Bank of Scotland. Despite the peacefulness of this scene, it is said that the road eventually became one of the busiest in Scotland. However, this changed when Lord James Douglas-Hamilton, Scottish Minister for Roads and Transport, opened the 5½ mile long Stepps bypass on 8 June 1992.

BOWLING GREEN STEPPS.

Stepps Bowling Club, originally Stepps & District Bowling Club, was formally opened on 10 June 1905 by Col. Alexander Sprot of Garnkirk. The ground for the club, together with £20 towards costs, had been gifted by Col. Sprot's wife with one condition attached – that her husband was made a life member! Shown here is the first clubhouse, which lasted until 1921 when a new one was opened by the wife of the then president, William Watson. The clubhouse was extended in the 1960s, but in 1987 the entire building was demolished and another one built to replace it. This was opened by Mrs Florence Boyce, the wife of a former president. Through the trees can be glimpsed some of the houses on Lenzie Road, a number of which are over a hundred years old.

OPENING OF STEPPS RECREATION GROUND - 29·6·10·

There was cause for celebration on 29 June 1910 when the new Stepps Public Park was declared open by Col. Alexander Sprot. Initially, proposals to establish a park had been bedevilled by disagreements, but with the establishment of a Trust (supported by a donation of £100 from the Colonel), the project was able to proceed. As can be seen from this photograph, the event was well-supported and no doubt the spectators enjoyed the ensuing programme of music which was supplied by the boys from Mossbank Industrial School. In time the park became the accepted venue for various community events and special occasions, such as the 1946 Welcome Home ceremony when local returning servicemen were publicly thanked for their service during the Second World War and each presented with a £5 note.

When this view of Anniesdale Avenue was taken in 1919 it had been laid out for almost a decade. The terraced houses on the right, and the larger property on the left called Hillburn (all still standing), were fairly typical of the style of house being built at the turn of the twentieth century, as were the houses on Lenzie Road, just visible in the far distance. Perhaps the most distinguished building in Anniesdale Avenue was Stepps United Free Church (later St Andrew's Church), which stood at the junction with Blenheim Avenue. However, after its congregation merged with that of Whitehill Parish Church to form Stepps Parish Church in 1983, the building was sold and later demolished to allow the construction of new flats at Blenheim Court.

STEPPS U.F. CHURCH.

Stepps United Free Church originated as a mission station for Millerston United Free Church, and became a preaching station in June 1905. A year later the United Free Hall was opened, the memorial stone of which was laid by Sir William Bilsland, Lord Provost of Glasgow. The congregation remained determined to erect a church, however, and this finally came to fruition when a memorial stone was laid on 22 June 1912. The church was built at a cost of £5,000 and opened on 14 June 1913. A few months later, in November, a new church hall was also opened after the original one had been damaged by fire earlier in the year. In 1929, when the United Free and Established Churches in Scotland reunited, it was agreed to retain both buildings but change the name of the United Free Church to St Andrew's. Sadly, both St Andrew's and its hall have now been demolished.